To my family and my best friends
(past and present – you know who you are!)

Laura's Diary

ORANA
PUBLISHING

First published in Great Britain in 2006 by Orana Publishing Limited
www.oranapublishing.com

A CIP catalogue record for this book is available from the British Library.

ISBN 10: 0-95507-512-2
ISBN 13: 978-0-9550751-2-4

Cover design and typesetting by Reluctant Hero
www.reluctanthero.co.uk
With thanks to Sarah Jane Claydon

Printed and bound in the United Kingdom by Mackays of Chatham.

CONTENTS.

FINAL THOUGHTS

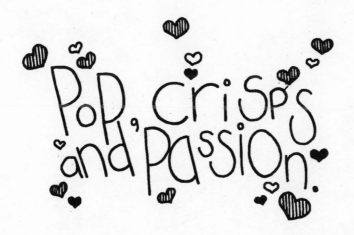

23rd July 1993.

Dear Diary,

Went to Youth Club. I really fancy Jamie. He sat next to me in the Pool room and his leg was touching my knee.
I was in heaven.
Josie and Matt were snogging all night. I might get a boyfriend soon

Also played in a netball match - lost 22·0

Love Laura ♡
x

Laura luvs Jamie

28th August 1993.

Dear Diary,

School is pretty boring. Got up to submarine level on Nadine's game boy.

Had a dream about Jamie last night. It was so real. I looked into his eyes and we kissed.

I love him, he's just so nice....

..oh

I daydream about him. I try to look my best and act cool around him. I just hope he likes me.

Everytime I hear
"Boom Shake the Room"
I think of him
                    Love Laura x

30th August 1993.

Dear Diary,

Did the papers with Becky. There were 5 leaflets. Lucy told me she started her period but I don't believe her. Last night I went on a ghost walk it was a real laugh. Jamie was so quiet but so cute. He always walked near me in the scary bits and he touched my arm. I always seem to get enough guts to say something to him the next day after I've seen him. He makes me feel all warm in places I never knew existed kate told me Jamie told Andy I've got nice eyes - oh well I suppose that's something anyway.

Write soon

Love laura xxx

❋ 1st September 1993.

Dear Diary,

Daddy says I'm using too much electricity and I have to turn my radio alarm clock off at night. If I'm late for school its his bloody fault

Been thinking about Jamie alot. Maybe I should ask him out? Its just such a lot counting on it.
Will everyone at Youth club tease me? Will Jamie dump me after going out with me for about 1 hour then totally ignore me?

✂ ✂ ✂

Should I wait for the right time (like soon) or after Christmas?
Wouldn't it be ace if I could find out if he likes me? He could have told Andy, he did say I've got nice eyes after all.
If he doesn't love me then why am I reading the signs wrong? I'm confused...

Love Laura x

7½ STONE.

6th September '93

Dear Diary,
 Got told off in French for doodling on my Tricolor. Madam Martin said I was defacing school property. I only wrote 'Jamie' really small.
 She hates me anyway.
Decided I can't wreck my friendship with Jamie by saying something. I'd rather have him as a mate than nothing at all. I can love him secretly.

Oh I don't know what to do? I'm sorry if I repeat myself but its the things that mean a lot to me that I repeat.
 I don't want people to guess how I'm feeling. I'm trying to be subtle but I love him or like him so much. Its not easy

Love Laura

P.S. Got weighed and measured at school. I weigh 7½ stone + have grown 1 inch.

9th September 93

Dear Diary,
Now I know why Jamie
was quiet on the Ghost walk. Becky
told me today that Jamie had
told Andy I had a nice body
(in other words he likes me!)
Becky told everyone. Jamie got
embarrassed and said he didn't
like me anymore and denied the
whole thing.
I hope this hasn't made us drift
further apart. I can't believe that
he actually said he fancies me!
(kind of) ME!!!

Becky kept teasing me about it
and I got embarrassed
To Top it off Mama made toffee.
Ralph and Henry have been
stealing it but I got blamed

Love Laura x

13th September 93.

Dear Diary,

Today I finished the 3b test in Maths, went into town and bought some new felt tips.

I can't wait to see Jamie again.

I had another dream about him last night and we were goin' steady and we F.kissed! Oh god I really want to go out with him.

I just hope that what everyone says about him liking me is true.

Feeling sorry for me yet?

I really do totally fancy Jamie.

I keep hearing his laugh and his voice in my head -

Jamie
❤ + ❤
ME

hes so cute!!!

Anyway see you soooooooooon

Love Laura
X x x

*
 * *
  * *
Dear Diary, ❀   14th September 1993.

Today I skived swimming. Got told
off by Mrs Hartley in Music +
two girls got sent home for
experimenting with cannabis.

Jamie took me up knavesmire with
the lads. The fair's in York. Got
dead nervous in case he tried to
kiss me. It says in magazines
just to relax and go with the
flow. but what if its not
that simple? Are there rules?!?

Jamie let me wear his coat on the
way home. He wears Lynx deodorant
Africa - he's so trendy.

Daddy fined me a weeks pocket money
coz I didn't untie my shoes but I
did get £5 from Nana + Grandad
for my exam results.

Speak soon
Laura xxx

Exam Results

ENGLISH 85% – I am very pleased with my result 3% off the top mark

MATHS 70% – Highest was 81% + Ruth got that.

HISTORY 66% – Lauren's upset. She got below 50% Highest was 90%. I beat Zoe, she's a bit pissed off.

RE 89% – Highest was 93%. I'm really pleased with it. Mrs Knight said she was pleased.

GEOGRAPHY 73% – very pleased. Got the same mark as Mary T + she's a geek I got B2. YEAH!

ART 85% – Really pleased Highest was 89% 4 off.

SCIENCE 89% – Don't know what highest is but really pleased GOT A1

FRENCH 82% - V. pleased. One of highest in div.
Might move up

GERMAN 78% - Got more than I expected. Same mark as Zoe in oral

Music 70% - Got higher mark than most people in Orchestra

HA!

Love Laura xxx

20th September

Dear Diary,

I looked up Jamie in the phonebook + now I know his number AND address - weeney good !!!
I wish we went out but i would hardly see him, well I could on Fridays If he met me after hockey practice.
I tried ringing him 3 times he answered once and said he'd ring me back an hour ago. Now he's not answering I think his phone might be broken.

Maybe he doesn't like me ....

...oh sorry for rambling on.

The trip to Megabowl has been Cancelled so I won't be able to see him till tomorrow.

Just watched Quantum leap I love that programme

Anyway speak to you tomorrow
Lauraxxx

21st September.

Dear Diary,

This is the worst day ever - I cut my toe after swimming AND my finger. Lucy was in a mood with me when I hadn't even done anything wrong - cow. Then, to top it all off, I was meant to go to youth club but Daddy has grounded me because I had my bedside lamp on when it was still daylight outside.

I haven't seen Jamie for 3 days!! This is so unfair!

Sometimes I really wish I was adopted. He doesn't know what its like, I just want to get away from this place. It's now 10.30pm and I've been up all this time thinking about it... well the course of true love never does run smooth. I hope he doesn't forget about me .... Laura x

Dear Diary * 29th September.'
* Got my hair cut at 4:30.
I saw 7 shooting stars last night
and wished on everyone of
them that Jamie would go out with
me. He's been ignoring me. I
just don't understand. We were
getting on so well. Its so hard.
He's just turning his feelings on+
off like a light.
    Got youth club tonight. I'm going
to offer everyone a sweet round
apart from him, and he'll say
something about me not offering
him one and then I'll say —
    You shouldn't take sweets from
Strangers, maybe you should get
to know me a bit better first!

Mary drew on my homework.
I HATE   HER
she's so annoying + ginger   x x
    I'll talk soon   x x x
                        Love Laura x
                        x

I HATE HER

I HATE HER

I hate her...
I hate her
I hate her
I hate her
. I hate her

I HATE HER

I hate her

Ginger Hair

I HATE HER

30th September 93

Dear Diary,

I just got back from Youth Club. Things weren't good at the beginning of the night ~~Ja~~ Jamie wasn't talking to me, he was ignoring me. I was really upset and making lots of effort to talk to him I'm sorry about my writing but I'm veeerey ~~tired~~ tired.

We had a leaf fight on the way home. It was a good laugh. Then Jamie started singing 'tell Laura I love her' and someone said 'go on then' but I took no notice. Kate asked me if I was going to ask him out, but I think that if Jamie really likes me then he'll get the guts to ask me out plus its kind of the boys job. See ya

Love Laura xx

P.S. Rachel G is really good at netball. I have to play better or she'll get centre.

♡ ♡ ♡   4th October 93.

Dear Diary, ♡ ♡
   ♡ Ruth's hamster is still missing
She's quite upset. Looked for it in the
Junior Science lab but I think it
   might be dead.
Got some new perfume from the Body
Shop. It smells nice and I also got some
kiwi lip balm. WEENEY excited
bout tonight. It's Diane's birthday
party in town. All the possy are
going, should be a laugh
            I'm going to wear :
                  BLACK SHORT SKIRT
                    BLACK TIGHTS
          MAROON SWEATER SHOP JUMPER
                  MY KICKERS .
I've decided to dance really near the
DJ so Jamie will be able to see me .
I think it might happen tonight.
Bit worried bout my brace OH-
I just LOVE him So much ♡ ♡
   ♡ I'll write and tell you what
                         happens...

            love Laura xxxx

5th October 1993.

Dear Diary,

6 days till my Birthday. Got an 'A' for my technology project. I feel a bit forlorn. The party didn't go the way I wanted. Sarah got really drunk, was sick all over her top and on Andys shoes and Alan had to take her home. Jamie looked really cute but he didn't talk to me all night. I cried in the toilets but I don't think anyone noticed. The whole possy walked home together, me and Andy hung back. He's so nice. He was being really sweet and told me not to worry about Jamie.

Don't quite know how it happened but he held my hand and I got off with him on the bridge.

Think it went Ok.
My breathing went a
bit funny and I got all
hot, and I ended up getting chewing
gum on my coat !!!

I just feel so guilty. Can you love
two people at the same time?
I can't stop thinking about it

At least I'll know what to
do when I snog Jamie

Oh I'm so confused.

Love
Laura
xxx

October 12th.

Dear Diary,

Found out I got the part in the school play - Its James + the Giant Peach. I'm the Centipede. Went to Youth Club. Jamie + Andy were there. I still don't know what to do. Do you think Jamie knows? or anyone else??

Sarah was being mean to me for wearing a body top. She said it was tarty. She kept talking about it behind my back, but I saw her.

Ended up playing spin the bottle upstairs. There were loads of us Jamie was opposite me and Andy was two people to the right.

I really hoped it would land on me.

Jamie looked really cute in his cap. It landed on Ben 3 times!!!
He had to kiss
        Gemma
        Lisa +
            Emma,

Then Norma came up and confiscated the bottle she said it was for our own good. In her experience spin the bottle tended to get out of hand

COW that could have been my chance!

Sometimes I think it will never happen. I don't know what to do. At least Jamie spoke to me but Andy is so nice as well and he could be my boyfriend now because we kissed. My heart is so confused
        Oh what should I do?
                Love Laura xx

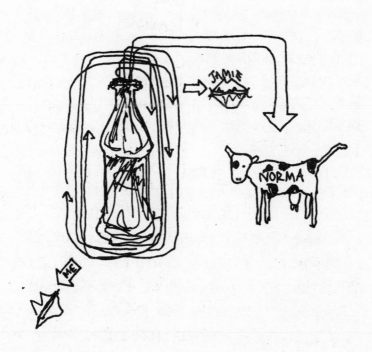

October 14th

Dear Diary,

Sprained my wrist again in hockey and have to wear a support. Chain came off my bike on the way home from school. I decided this was fate. It meant I should walk the long way home and try and find the boys. I walked passed Jamie's house, went to the shop, then walked past his house again and then went to see if they were playing footie on the field, then to see if they were playing basketball.

I didn't see them.

Daddy fined me a weeks pocket money for leaving my hair dryer plugged in. I think I'm love sick my heart aches for both of them, surely one of them will be my boyfriend?

I always thought I'd have one by now. Speak soon
Love Laura xxx.

October 16th 1993.

Dear Diary,
          I was ill today and Mama bought
me some strepsils. Becky came round
to see me because she owed me 2 quid.
I've decided I still like Jamie. I couldn't
stop thinking about him today.
I put 'Boom Shake the room' on
repeat in my room. I keep trying to
picture his face in my mind. I really
need a photo coz I can only picture
parts of his face... like I can always
remember his hair and mouth but
I can't remember his eyes and nose.
Maybe I'm not good enough for him
I haven't got the looks or personality
to match him. I'll understand if he
doesn't want to go out with me.. and
its really pointless me writing this stuff
really. Went to bed early coz daddy's
friend came to stay from Canada and
I didn't like him. CU soon
     love from a very lovesick, distressed +
                    hassled   Laura xx

October 24th

Dear Diary,
I'm so sorry I haven't written for so long but such a lot has been going on. Last Saturday was the sleep out to raise money for the homeless at Youth club. It was **MEGA** good!!! I ended up sleeping

next to Jamie.
Jamie started holding my hand and I was dead suprised when we started hugging like this....

I ♥ Jamie
(I.D.S.T)

Then when we lay down he put his arm round me. He's so cute. I'm glad it was dark so he couldn't see me blush. Lisa was teasing us Jamie told her to leave us alone. He moved closer to me and then he came in my box

I couldn't believe it !!!!

It was the best night of my life
♡Love Laura xx♡

October 26th

Dear Diary,
          Went to the dentist and had
my brace tightened up. It hurt.
Mrs Davey wasn't there for Geography
and I saw a ghost in English.
          Kate came round and we talked
about the lads. I'm worried that
Saturday night might have been a
one off. Kate said maybe Jamie
was playing me around + leading
me on.

Oh. I really hope he isn't but she's
probably right. Maybe I'm better off
sticking to Andy after all. Everyone at
school is sick of me talking about him
I know it sounds stupid but even
thinking about him gives me
Goosebumps. I don't know what to do
Maybe I should go out with Andy,
   he only lives 3 minutes away
          from me..
                    love laura x x x

	Jamie	David	Paul	Ben	Andy
Looks	4	1	2	3.5	3
Personality	4	2	3	3.5	3.5
Niceness	2.5	3	2	3.5	4
Hugability	4.5	1	2	3.5	4.5
Snogability	4.5	1	2	3	3.5
Talkability	2	1	2	3	4
Sportiness	4	1	3	2.5	4
Trendiness	4.5	2.5	4	3.5	4
Could I see Them?	1	2.5	1	2.5	4
TOTAL	31	15	21	28.5	34.5

October 29th 93.

Dear Diary,

☆OH MY GOD!!!

Just got back from **THE** most
amazing night in my ~~entire~~
life !!!   I'm so happy !!!
I can't stop smiling !! ☺

 I feel like I am floating and my
heart is kind of fluttering.
Its past my curfew, I just got in. I'll
probably get grounded or fined
but I don't even care. Had a
disco at Youth club. It was ACE!
 Got on really well with Jamie all night
Then when they put Whitney Houston
on for the last dance he came
and found me. EVERYONE was
looking but I didn't care. He had his
hands on my bum + I had mine

round his neck. I was dead nervous.
Then I actually....

GOT OFF WITH JAMIE !!

My teeth tuched his twice and
his tongue tasted of Salt + Vinegar
Crisps

I liked it !!

I just can't believe it !!!!/!!

Wishes do come true

I LAURA SAYERS
HAVE SNOGGED
JAMIE
IDST

love laura
x x x

November 5th 93.

Dear Diary,
 I'm saving up for the German exchange
Got 23 quid so far. Got told off in RE
for talking. Its been 7 days now since I got
off with Jamie. Went to see the
fireworks at Cliffords tower tonight. All
the possy were there apart from Jamie.
Andy said he was doing his homework.
Since when has Jamie done homework?
He wasn't at youth club on Monday either.
I really hope he's not avoiding me. I feel
really sad. Lisa + Ben were being all
lovey dovey all night. I wanted to be
like that with Jamie. All snuggly with
his arms around me, watching the
fireworks all romantic. I think he's
regretting what happened. Maybe I can't
kiss properly + he noticed. Its just not fair
but I knew it was too good to be true...
+ I've got loads of homework to do
     Maybe jamie will be out
          tomorrow
          Speak soon love laura
                          x

Dear Diary,   November 7th 93.

I'm sorry if my writings a bit funny but I'm really tired, upset and just want to die.
Saw Jamie on the way home from school, he was walking past the park with a girl. She was holding his hand. I just cycled past as fast as I could... got home + cried

I can't even stop

Becky says she's going out with him and she's called Gemma and goes to his school.

WHY HAS THIS HAPPENED?!? Everything was going so well and now she's come + ruined

EVERYTHING

She's not even pretty anyway. I
might as well not bother anymore,
whats the point?
He's not worth it if he's going to
treat me like that.

Andy would never do that
Andy would never do that
Andy would NEVER do that

Im so upset
I feel all empty
love Lauraxxx

P.s. Ruth dyed her hair black
     its gone a bit wrong
        + looks stupid.

Jamie?

Andy?

November 10th '93

Dear Diary,
    Had to take all my friendship bands off in P.E coz Miss Robinson said they were dangerous and Daddy fined me a weeks pocket money for lying down in the lounge. He said I shouldn't treat the house like a gymnasium. Still gutted about Jamie, still can't believe it but I don't think I've got any tears left. My heart feels all cold like ice. Gemma can have him she'll probably get dumped soon anyway coz thats what he's like. I decided. I liked Andy again but I phoned him tonight + now he's being funny with me too. This was NOT meant to happen. Everything is going WRONG! I just want someone to love me. I want a boyfriend like everyone else. I want to be normal but that looks like it's never going to happen. Sorry, I'm crying again. I'll probably be by myself forever No one wants me Laura x

November 15th '93

Dear Diary,
   Had to spend 6 quid of the money
I saved for the German exchange
  (keep getting fined) Scored two goals
in hockey but we still lost. Its been
8 days since I found out about Jamie
I still feel really sore. It just makes me
feel so upset when I think about all
the good times we had and how he
made me feel so special. How can the
same person make you feel so happy
and then so sad?
          Why did no one tell me?
I read in my magazine that you can't
just sit around   waiting for 'him'
to come along. Enjoy yourself,
you only live once   after all!
Sometimes I would really like a
boyfriend and crave for one if you like
and feel lonely , but other times....

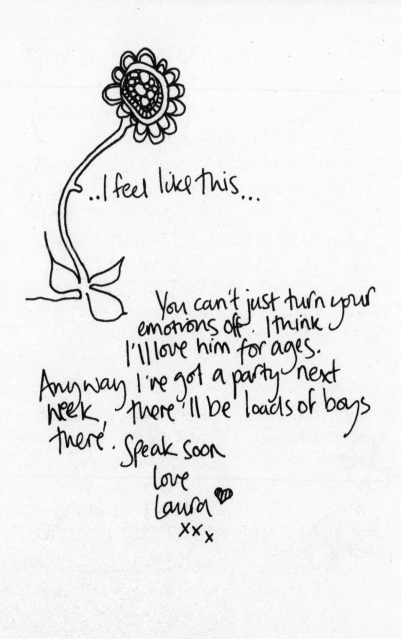

...I feel like this...

You can't just turn your
emotions off. I think
I'll love him for ages.
Anyway I've got a party next
week, there'll be loads of boys
there'. Speak soon
                love
                Laura ♥
                xx x

CODES

WHF = Water her flower

LMF = love me forever

SHP = Sing his Praises

THUTA = Take me up the aisle

IMSH = I must see him

BSMBH = Be still my beating heart

8th April 1996

Dear Alice,
It was a charity day today at College and we had to pay 25p to Unicef. Sarah has got the BIGGEST spot on her forehead. My skin is quite clear at the moment -

HA HA !.

Got told off twice in German coz Mrs Thompson came back in and caught me whistling at boys out of the window. Apparently if I put as much concentration into my work as I do messing about I would be an A grade student. Then at dinner Daddy fined me a weeks pocket money for shoveling my food and had to eat the rest with a dessert fork.
Sometimes Adults are so lame.

Anyway got to go coz Anthony's
coming over at 7 for my
piano lesson and I have to
go freshen up and practice
before he gets here

Love
Laura
x
x
x x

9th April 1996.

Dear Alice,
    I can't seem to do anything right at the moment. College is pretty dull. Got tons of English course work to do and I think I am coming down with a sore throat.

My piano lesson went well though. Anthony is teaching me Bach's Prelude Number **1**. He says my hand movement is really coming on. He just really gets me. Probably cos he's well young compared to my other teachers, and he's well good looking. He really listens to me, and he's really sophisticated and mature compared to the lads I know.

    ... Oh, by the way, Emma says she let Simon W.H.F. I don't believe her.

Speak to you soon
love Laura
xx

15th April 1996.

Dear Alice,
    Miss Robinson was in a right mood
today and me + Zoe have been expelled
from the team. They'll probably lose
now anyway. Also got an A for my
leaf montage in Art.
Had another lesson with Anthony. I'd
been looking forward to it all week.
I love the way he closes his eyes
whilst I play. He says that I'm
really coming along and that I've
mastered the right hand and I have
just got to bring my left up to scratch.

He stayed and talked to me for half an
hour after the lesson finished. He kinda
had smiley eyes and I got a bit embarrassed
if I look at him for too long. He likes
Shed Seven too and said he'd seen
Rick Witter in the Cross Keys in town.
    I might go there
        I think he likes me ♡
            love laura x

16th April 1996.

Dear Alice,
    Just got in from town. My coat
stinks of cigarettes but I sprayed
myself with deo before I got in
+ I think I've got away with it.

Went to the Cross keys in town,
    Rick Witter wasn't there.
        Neither was Anthony - Boo..!!

I decided I really like him today,
    Anthony that is, not Rick Witter

I talked to Emma about it and she
says go for it. I don't think my
mum would mind, she seems
    to like him alot too.

I got Emma to call in his work and
ask if he was seeing anyone,
and guess what...
                they said he wasn't.
I just need him to notice me
He's just so niiiiiiiiiiiiiice

          Love,
            Laura
                    xxx

LAF

Monday 18th April 1996

Dear Alice,
        I decided to put "sun-in" in my
hair. I want to see if blondes really
do have more fun. And I've come up
with a plan. I need to get Anthony
out in a situation where I can show
him that I'm not just good at playing
the piano if you know what I mean..?
There's a Shed Seven concert at
the Barbican next week and there's
still tickets available.. I can't believe it!

Baby sitting = £10.00
Savings = £5.00   but I owe Emma £5.00
Pocket money = £10.00   + love   £500

TOTAL = £15 £10
        need extra 10

If I babysit on Wednesday and
I don't get fined again I should have
enough for tickets cos you can get a
discount with a York card.
        Then I can give two tickets to him
so he can go with a mate, and
then I can bring Emma and we're

both got back up.
I'll give them to him as a present
and say that if he wants to meet
before hand then that would be cool.

Im so excited *
I always think about him
in bed at night *

Just hope this works *

love

Laura
xx

Friday 22nd April 96

Dear Alice, I think today is possibly the best day of my life. First off the team lost 14-0 in the match today! And ANTHONY AGREED TO GO TO THE GIG WITH ME!

He came round to my lesson but I couldn't concentrate cos he kept touching my arm, and I could feel him breathing near me. . But I don't care if I never play the piano again. I gave him the tickets and he says we should definitely meet up before the gig.

I think he might actually like me !! ♥♥

...ME!

if he brings a good looking mate
Emma might even get off with
him.
I'm so happy I could cry!

I think he might be the one!
What am I going to wear
Alice?

LMF WMF SHP
TAUT A
IMSH

love laura
xx

P.S. Anthony says the 'Sun In'
that I put in my hair looks, and
I quote 'really cute!'

28th April 1996.

Dear Alice,

Had a family meeting today because 10 quid has gone missing from Mama's purse. Whoever it was has until tomorrow at 6pm to own up (I think it was Henry) My hair is looking really blonde now and my tape recorder is broken so I have to listen to the radio. Anthony just called he was on the phone to my Mum for ages before she passed it over. They must have been sorting out payment for my lessons or something

Things just get better + better. His mate can't make it anymore. Its just going to be him and us. Its practically a proper date !!! I just tried on my outfit and ♡♡♡ practiced my makeup * I know this is meant to be. 👄 * I can just feel it
love Laura ♡
xx

Ps: BSMBH ♡

29th April 1996

Dear Alia,

Its 5 past 7. I was ready and set 5 minutes ago. Perfect make up, hair flicked out — looking quite good for me. Anthony just called.

He asked if ~~we~~ everything was still ok for tonight and double checked we're meeting in the Punch Bowl, and then asked me if it was ok if he brought someone else? He asked if he could bring his girlfriend!

His GIRLFRIEND !!

I think I want to die!
It feels like my heart is actually breaking...

So much for perfect make up! I look a mess, my eyes are black and I can ~~hardly~~ hardly see through my tears to write this!

I really thought he was the one,
but all this time he was
leading me on and just wanted to
use me for my Shed Seven tickets.

There's no way I can go now,
and I can never play the
piano again!

 It'll always remind me
of him and the love
we once had

love
laura
x

When someone that you love has to go,
the feelings from your heart melt) like snow
Everything you have turns to stone,
and you take seperate paths this time alone.
The distance may be far like earth + the moon,
but maybe we'll be together sometime
                                    (soon,)

Anytime you need me
              I'll be there,
I'll comfort you, stand by you and
              take away your fears.

When the friendship that we had breaks
              like glass,
And the tears that slowly full fade + pass,
My hearts forever yours + your friend.
I'll love you eternally,
              now until the end.

Friday 29th Aug 1997.

Dear Diary,
          Just got back from the hotel,
we're full at the moment cos of the
races. Jean's being a right cow
and got in a right mard cos I
forgot to put a new bin bag in rm15.
Lynne said not to take any notice. Henry
just got back from the U2 concert
at Roundhay Park. He went with
the rest of 'Monster Sunshine'.

He just told me that Ben (lead guitar)
kept talking about me in the car on
the way back and that he fancies me!

I don't even remember what he looks
    like!

I didn't want to ask Henry too much
  in case I looked too keen.

Apparently I met him before at the last

Amnesty concert but all I can remember
is there's one that looks like a
teradactil.
                    I hope its not him..
I could really do with a boyfriend, I think
I've really   still got a lot to learn.
                          love...

                    Laura   x x x

Sunday 31st Aug 1997.

Dear Diary,
           I'm at the hotel tonight.
Just locked up. Room 3 are a
complete nightmare. They stayed in
the bar for ages. They've got a
really annoying kid   who kept
climbing on the bar stools and f'ingering
all the brass.... and when I told it
not to it just pretended to be a teletubby.
Anyway I'm in bed now and guess
who called me tonight?

"..BEN.."

It was well embarrassing cos I answered
the phone with the whole
                     'Good evening the holgate
              hotel, Laura speaking.
               How can I help you?'

but he just thought it was funny!

We're going to meet on Wednesday at 8pm
in the ✗ keys. His mate Calum is
coming too ✗ but that's ok cos I
know ✗ him and I hate going into
pubs by myself and trying ✗ to find
people...... and I still ✗ can't remember
what Ben looks like so at least I'll
recognise Callum. To be honest he doesn't
have to be that nice, just average would
do.
 I hope he doesn't think I'm weird cos
I drink pints... maybe I should drink
halves? Then I'll ✗ look more classy !!!
I actually went to the football yesterday
with Henry cos he said Ben would be
there ✗ but he wasn't so I left after
Richard Cresswell got sent off cos he was
the only one with decent legs.
On breakfasts tomorrow then I'm going
to Marks + Spencers to get some new ✗
underwear for uni - ✗ might even need
 it sooner! Can't wait til Wednesday
                  love Laura xxx

Wednesday 3rd Sept 1997.

Dear Diary,
    Just got in from town. Daddy just
came in and told me off for playing my
music when I didn't even have any
on! He said I'd wake up Mary but
he did that quite successfully by having
a go? I saw Jamie on the iron bridge
on the way to town. I haven't seen
him for ages. He asked where I was going
so I told him and he said I looked
gorgeous. It felt good cause I knew I
    did!! Anyway I just met BEN ♡
The evening went very well—
thankfully. Ben wasn't the one that
looked like a teradactil.!! He's got
dark hair. He was wearing red trousers
and a checked shirt and kept playing
with a silver plectrum he had on a
chain round his neck.. A true guitar
player!!!
   ♡♡♡

Calum kept going off to play pool by himself. I kept catching Ben looking at my cleavage but he said he was admiring my necklace! When Calum went Ben started touching my leg under the table It was nice...

We decided to go back to his for a bit. He introduced me to his mum and then we went to mess around in his room for a bit

Ben's mum gave me a real look as I left .. So I just smiled sweetly ☺

I got a massive blister on the side of my foot from wearing my Spice Girls boots but I've just popped it.. and anyway it was worth it!!!!
love
Laura xxx

Monday 8th September 1997

Dear Diary,

Just got in and I'm absolutely knackered cos I stayed at Ben's house last night!

Not properly though, there were a few of us there, including Henry who went back after their gig so we couldn't really do much!

They played the Winning Post, not many people turned up, but I thought they were brilliant!!!

They played a lot of their own stuff + did a really cool cover of the Foo Fighters 'My poor Brain'...
I think it's an album track!

Ben thanked me for being there, winked at me and dedicated a song to... * Laura his *'Girlfriend'* *

It was *so* romantic and I felt so proud. Pity there weren't more people there to witness it!
Ben held my hand all the way back to his, he was being very sweet. He stopped me by the river, kissed me for ages and then took off his necklace and gave me the plectrum. He said he wanted me to wear it.
I couldn't believe it, it felt so significant!
He's just such a nice guy and there's so many funny coincidences its unbelievable

♥ He's football captain + I was hockey captain

♥ His birthday is the 10th October + mine is the 11th

♥ And we both really like Oasis!

What am I going to do when I go to Uni?
love laura

Ps. the tamagotchi I got him died.

Thursday 11th September 97.

Dear Diary, Sorry I haven't written for a while but I've been at the hotel for the last few nights. Finally got my address through for Uni after the mix up.. its Murano St Student Village, Lennox House, Flat D room 5. It all seems very real now and I'm a bit scared. Only a week to go now... Been seeing a LOT of Ben.. ok all of him a lot HA.HA. HA.

I called him on Wed from work and jokingly said he should come and stay. I was just finishing the kalamazoo when he turned up in Reception. I couldn't believe it !!! He was wearing that aftershave° that I like and his white YSL shirt. He helped me lock up and then we went

up to the flat. Its really cool having
that place .. we can do what we want
up there and its really private. It was
embarrassing coz I hadn't shaved
but he didn't seem to mind.
  We were just getting into things
when I had to go down onto the
second floor as the bath was
  leaking in Rm 12. Luckily rm 10
was free so I moved them in there,
but when I got back to the flat Ben
had fallen asleep.
It was funny cos I had to sneak him
out first thing in the morning
without anyone seeing —

            but I think we ..
            got away with it

Jane's just called and told me
  that her and Seggy are going
to take me up to Glasgow...

Really nice of them. I just know
I'm going to be really upset —
I'll miss Ben so much
+ I'll miss the next Monster Sunshine
gig.
love

Laura xx

P.s. Ben sent me flowers at
the hotel this morning
— none of the girls said
anything but I
can tell they were
jealous!

Friday 12th September

Dear Diary,

So— apparently Ben didn't send me the flowers yesterday. I gave him a massive hug to say thanks today and he didn't know what I was on about. I phoned the hotel to see if they knew anything and little Claire said she'd put the card in the handover book for me so it didn't get lost. She read it to me over the phone and it turns out it was from Mr Thomas - a guy who stayed in Room 7 a couple of weeks ago.

Ben was not impressed. He accused me of flirting with the guests and said he couldn't trust me, then went in a sulk. When I tried to explain that being nice to the guests was part of my job but he just ignored me

and continued his game on the
Nintendo — so I came home.
That was about 3pm and its now
9pm. I just tried phoning him to
talk about it and his mum said he
wasn't there. Apparently he's gone
out with Calum and Jenny
        (who he used to go out with!)
I know she still likes him...
        ..you can tell.
What makes it worse is that he
gave her a plectrum too.. and
                she still wears it!

I really hope nothing happens. I don't
want it to end like this before Uni.
The annoying thing is that I haven't
done anything wrong. He's being really
childish — I didn't think the age
gap would matter but I'm obviously
much more maturer than he
I wish he'd call...   Laura x

Tuesday 16th September '97

Dear Diary,

I'M GOING TO UNI TOMORROW!

Went to the hotel to say bye and hand in my uniform and the girls had got me a leaving present, really sweet of them... a pan set and a book of the karma Sutra!

Spent most of the day packing up the last of my stuff. It's funny looking at most of your life packed up into boxes. Daddy told me off as I stacked everything by the door, he said it was blocking the heat from the radiator and that I might as well burn £5 notes to keep warm. So I went and had a cigarette outside where he could see...
.. just to piss him off and
Mark my independence!

HA HA.

My room looks pretty empty. Mary
has been crying alot as
she doesn't want me to go.
Ben still hasn't called .. I've left
messages but I think its over.
I can take a hint
I just hope he's not back with
Jenny.....
.. It would kill me to see them
two together..

She's a Slag anyway

What makes it worse is that I just
found a note in my coat pocket from
last week. Its from Ben. Its
from the gig and says he's so glad
he met me & that he really likes
me. Made me cry and feel
sick when I saw it. Been listening
to my new Oasis album alot —
there's a song on it called "Don't go Away"

... Thats how I want Ben to feel about me.

Mama got me a new poster for my room in Glasgow. Its a 'No Fear' one that says

"don't let your fears stand in the way of your dreams"

I think its really meaningful and really represents my life

I hope I'll be ok
love

Laura xx

Wednesday 17th September �֍
1997
Dear Diary,
        What a weird day....
I'm sitting on my bed in my new
room. It's ok, . quite small but I've
got my own 'sink'. There's a big
kitchen with places to sit a shower
and two toilets

    No one else has moved in the flat
yet.. It's just me. I managed to hold
it together until Jane, Seggy +
Mama left. I didn't want them to
think that I couldn't handle it....
    but the truth is- I can't-
                    Its Horrible..
I'm in a strange room in a strange
place and I don't even know my
way to the nearest shop. For the
first time in my life York is a
long way away and I'm very much
                alone.

One good thing though is that
Ben came round to the house
this morning before I left. Mama
and Daddy gave us a bit of
space so we went up to my
room and chatted about things
before making the most of our
last ½ hour together before I had
to set off.

My duvet was all packed up so we
tried not to make too much of a
mess of Mary's bed!!

He gave me a tape he'd made, some
songs on it he sings. The sweetest
thing in the world...
                    It made me cry.

I've just got to be brave now.
I hope the people who move in will
                be nice
I hope I'll be ok.   love laura
                                xx

Tuesday 23rd Sept
1997

Dear Diary,
                Once again I'm writing
this because I can't get to sleep. The
people upstairs are   at it again.
            Don't they ever get tired?
They've been doing it for about an
hour now. Just when I think they've
stopped - the noises start again.
            It makes me feel a bit sick
        + it makes me miss Ben.
I don't know who they are. I think
it might be the guy   with the
denim jacket.   His girlfriend
looks like a slag.

Three Boys moved into the flat today
- so at least I'm not on my own.
But we've not spoken much -
        Probably because they're 4thyrs

and we don't have much in common.
And they smoke non-stop.

Dave came to talk to me yesterday
and suggested I move out cos he
doesn't think we're going to get
on.
   I've moved all my food out of
the kitchen in case they steal it.
But they're not the worst ones.
   Charlie is constantly waltzing into
my flat without knocking - so I've
started locking the door to keep
her out !!
      She's so loud
         I really hate her
And the guy from Portugal is really
giving me the creeps. I think
he fancies me. I'm trying not
to give him the wrong signals so
   I'm just being rude to him.

I met some lesbians today.
  They were in the laundry room
and started talking to me so I
ran away.

I want to go home but I know I
  can't. I really miss Ben. There's
always people on the phones and
even when you get on them you
can't talk privately. We were
trying to have an intimate conversation
but couldn't as people kept walking
past. So we've decided to start
  writing to each other as well
I hope some other first years move
  in soon ... this is crap.

      love

      Laura xx

Saturday 27th Sept 97

Dear Diary,

My head hurts I've just spent the last hour lying on the floor in the toilet but Charlie came in so I've locked myself in my room. Didn't make it to the toilet last night so my sink stinks...

and that bloody couple upstairs are at it again.

Seriously does she not get sore?!

Some new people moved in. They seem nice apart from one who wears a kagool all the time and another who has really flaky skin.

The lesbians cornered me in the laundry room yesterday and invited me out with them...

.. So I went out with the new
people instead.

Howie made Vodka jelly and I was
drunk before we even left the
building. I fell down the stairs on
the bridge leaving the village
and nearly died crossing the
main road.

Went to a pub called Crosslands where
some of Trainspotting was filmed
then ended up at 'Cheesy Pop'
at the QMU.

I got banned from the stage for
harassing DJ Toast and can't really
remember much after that apart
from the weird portugese guy
turning up smelling of garlic
and doing some weird dance
by me which involved him trying

to put his hands on my hips.

I tried to phone Ben last night when
I got back to tell him I miss him
but he didn't pick up.
He called earlier though and
shouted at me. His mum wasn't
very happy that I called at 4 in the
morning and I'm banned from
calling him now.
         He has to call me

    Its so unfair
    All I need is a cuddle and
    even my boyfriend hates me.
                    love
                    laura
                       x

    P.s. Got to matriculate
         on Monday

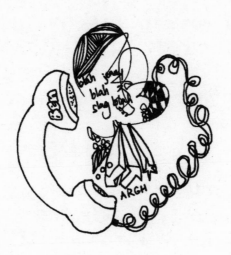

Tuesday 30th September
1997.

Dear Diary,
    I feel so Bad
    What have I done?

I've just got off with Alan. The boys
decided they wanted to get to
know me better. We started drinking
ages ago, we didn't have any mixers
so Dave just put everything we
had into a bucket.
I know thats not an excuse for doing
what I did but I feel so guilty.
    I can't tell Ben.
    He'd finish things on the spot-
but if I don't tell him will he notice
I'm acting funny?

Dave said its all fine and thats what
students are meant to do... but surely
the fact that I live with him is
    going to make things really
        awkward.

I managed to stop things before it got too out of hand... but the thing is, I was enjoying it.. and I'm tempted to go back and see him now!

I'm so confused.. Me and Ben were just going through a rough patch and perhaps Alan just gave me what I needed at the time?

Why do I always get myself into these situations ???

I'm meant to be going back to York for Ben's birthday so I can't tell him then, that would be a horrible thing to do.
Maybe I don't tell him anything?
He's not going to find out is he?

To top it off I collected my laundry this morning (the lesbians weren't there) and I must have left a sock in my white wash so now all my underwear is grey :. love laura xxx

Thursday 2nd October 97.

Dear Diary,
          I did it again.
I thought things were bad before
but I keep making things worse.
I got off with Alan again tonight!
He instigated it though so I'm not
to blame.

I'd been on the phone to Ben. I was going
to tell him about snogging Alan
   but he started going on about how
much of jenny he's been seeing...
   So I didn't. It makes me really
angry when he goes on about her.
He knows it upsets me and she's
such a stupid COW anyway
      I don't know why he likes her.
I was really upset by the end of the
call and Alan came into my room
to comfort me. He's really sweet

and made me feel better.
   One thing just kind of lead to
another.... it all seemed so
   natural.
Now my head is swimming with all
these thoughts and I feel guilt
beyond guilt.

I don't quite understand what it
all means... I'm not sure if I even
fancie Alan? Maybe he's more of
a playmate for when Ben's not here.

I feel torn. I really like Ben, when
we're not arguing we get on really
well but I'm sure he gets some
sick satisfaction from telling me
how many times he's taken Jenny
out. I would never do that to anyone.

GOD, why do I get myself into these
                    Situations?

P.S. I think my hair is   love laura xx
     falling out.

Thursday 9th October 1997.

Dear Diary,

My hair is definitely falling out.
I've got a little bald patch.

Alan and I had a talk. He says he's got
a lot of uni work on and that we
best nip the whole thing in the bud
before it all gets out of hand and
turns into anything else. I agree
but I hate it that he got to say
it first cos now I feel a bit rejected!

Anyway I'm going back to York this
weekend, its Ben's birthday tomorrow
and mines on Saturday. I've decided
to tell Ben what's happened,
hopefully he'll understand and
we'll be able to move on.

Bens having a party at the Bonding
Warehouse and I'm really looking
forward to snogging him at
every opportunity, just to make

Jenny jealous !!!
I can't wait !

Its a gangster and Molls party. Got no idea what to wear

What is a Moll anyway?

Obviously we can't use the hotel anymore so I've asked if Ben can stay at home with me. Mama asked me a loud of questions but I think she's coming around to the idea... on Saturday night Ben asked his mum if I can stay over, he's told her that my mums cool with it so hopefully it'll work.

I must remember to Shave !

Charlie moved out yesterday cos she said she wasn't bonding with people... glad she got the hint !

P.S. lisa + lin want me to go out with them on Weds + meet one of their friends. They reckon he's been on T.V. I think they're trying to set me up with him.

love

Laura x x

Sunday 13th October
1997.

Dear Diary,
Just on the train back
to Glasgow. I don't really want to go
back. Ben gave me one of his
jumpers so that I can smell him
but it just makes me want to cry.

Had such an excellent weekend.
Went straight to Ben's and had tea
with the family before the party,
but I didn't eat much cos I
was so nervous.

The party was really funny. Ben was
really tipsy before we got there and
was being really affectionate all
night. I knew Jenny was hating it
which made it even better.

She was doing the thing where
you pretend you're having a
really good time + kept looking
over to see if we'd noticed.

Ben + I snuck out half way through to
go and spend some time catching up
and stuff by the river but
Callum came and found us and
brought us back in cos people were
wondering where we'd gone.

Jenny stopped me in the toilets
and told me
            "It wouldn't last"
but that conversation was cut short
as she had to go and be sick!!!!!

            Silly Cow !!
JENNY!
IS A   I just left her to it.
BITCH!

We spent the rest of the weekend
   together. Daddy was in a mood cos
he said we were treating the house
like a knocking shop... but Ben
stayed anyway. He's got this new
   finger trick which is amazing!

I told him that I worried about Jenny
and that I'd been getting on really
well with Alan   at   Uni.
Ben told me Jenny was just a friend
and there's nothing to worry about.
He said he was   glad that   I was
making friends   and he can't wait
to meet Alan when he comes to stay.

I wanted to tell him I loved him but
thought I'd better not in case it was
    too soon.....
              ·· but I think I do..
          He's just so understanding

He got me the York City away strip
    for my birthday and Mama got
    me a new alarm clock

                        love
P.S. I don't think
he noticed my   Laura
bald patch.   xx

✧ ✦ Tuesday 15th October '97

Dear Diary, *✦*
✧

Just got in from Uni. I was really wet
 by the time I got in so I just changed
straight into my pyjamas
        (which are now grey)
Had my first theatre seminar with
   this graduate assistant called Matt.
You can tell all the girls fancy him
but I think he loves himself.
There's some properly weird people in
my group too.... Most of them
look like they need a good wash.
Matt said he wanted us to get rid of
our inhibitions... So we had to
pretend to be dinosaurs, a tree in
 a particular season and a utensil
you'd find in a kitchen.
     It's not really what I expected.

Met lisa + lin for lunch. They keep going on about this friend of theirs who they're trying to set me up with.

We're going out in Southside tomorrow with him and his mates. I'm not really bothered if he's famous or not to be honest.... my student loan just came in so I'm planning

a **big** me!

The warden's just been up to tell me to turn my music down. I only had it that loud cos the noises started again upstairs. That couple are really begining to gross me out... maybe I should contact the Guinness book of records?

It always makes me think about
Ben. He wrote me a dead nice
letter after I left and I got it
today. He says that Jenny's not
talking to him, that his mum
thinks I'm lovely and then it
all got a bit fruity towards
the end. I quite liked it and
I can't stop thinking about it

I miss him + I miss his touch

The boys have just got in so I might
go and see Alan in a bit.

love

Laura

x xxxxyxxxy

Thursday 17th October 97.

Dear Diary,

Just done the journey of shame back from Southside ... had to be back for my doctors appointment at 4pm.

Sleazy Alan, the portuguese guy was waiting for me in the kitchen when I got back. He said the fire alarm went off again really early this morning and he noticed I wasn't there and wanted to know where I'd been!! I got Dave and Alan to make him leave ... he's really odd and he always seems to be drinking milk!!

Had a really fun night actually. Met the guy Lisa + Lin were going on about. He's called Mr X and he used to be in ~~█████~~ I recognised him straight away but tried not to show it.

He's actually a really sweet guy, and we got on really well. Went to the 'Shed'. Lisa + Lin were pretending to be Australian all night trying to chat up these Rugby players which was very funny to watch, so I just stayed with Mr X.
I had to take my tights off half way through the night cos I got a massive ladder up my thigh. When I got back from the toilet Mr X made some comment about not wanting me to take them off as he wanted to climb it. I pretended I didn't hear him.

Lisa and Lin went home and I stayed at Mr X's flat... it's dead posh + his music collection is amazing. A loud of us went back. Nothing happened but I know it could have done if I'd pushed it... there were too many other people there anyway and I'm in love with Ben now so I did my best to act aloof..........

... I think it worked cos
he's asked to see me
again !

Maybe Uni isn't that bad
after all !

love

Laura xxx

P.S. Going to doctors now -
hopefully it'll be ok -
Maybe I've just been bleaching
it too much.

Monday 20th October 97.

Dear Diary,
          Just got a letter from Daddy
with an itemised phone bill from home
in it... He says he wants me to
contribute £73.46 towards it....

I'm going to double check it.

Mr X keeps calling but I keep missing
him. The last message he left said
he was going to be out of the country
next week so hopefully I'll see him
before then. Maybe I'll call him
tonight after I've called Ben. I can't
stop thinking about him.

Bit annoyed cos someone keeps nicking
my milk out of the fridge. I asked
the boys about it but they said
they knew nothing about it.

          I think its the weird
                    Portuguese guy.

Dave and Alan want to have a
Halloween party... I'm a bit dubious
cos all their friends are quite frankly,
weird. And the fire alarm is bound
to go off and I refuse to pay the fine...
especially after the phone bill
letter from daddy.

I've met a really nice girl called
Sarah who lives in the same flat
as the lesbians. She's really pretty,
got a really cool accent and is
going out with someone back home
too. We were talking about it all
last night and she understands how
hard it is. We ate loads of chocolate
checked each others backs for spots
and she lent me a counting crows
CD. I think she could be a really
good friend to me.

I started painting Ben a picture.
Haven't done any art for ages but
wanted to do something special

for him, especially after he made me that tape.

Its of two blue nudes and is coming on really well .....

maybe I'll give it to Mr X instead?

Got Hockey trials tonight for the Uni team.... hopefully I'll get in

Love

Laura xxx

P.S. picked up my prescription for my bald patch and its got steroids in it.

* * *
* ☆ * ☆ Tuesday 21st October 97.
Dear Diary, *
☆ ☆ *
☆ I just bought a train ticket. I've
decided I've had enough of uni. I'm
going to go home..... Tomorrow.
I miss Ben too much and its been
ages since we had any fun together.
Its so hard trying to keep a
relationship going over the phone,
especially when you're this much in
love ♡
♡ ♡
I've been listening to the CD Sarah
leant me a lot and 'Raining in
Baltimore' discribes my situation
exactly... apart from the fact its
about some town in America.

No one seems to understand how hard
it is for me being all alone in a place
you don't know: with people you
don't know...

There's only so many times you can say Auntie Ruby's coming to stay to avoid going out with them.

Me and Sarah were talking and she says she's going home and suggested I do the same.
       Its not like I'm going to miss much here... I can get the notes I miss, I'm sure I can practice being a dinosaur in my own time If I need to .. and Mr X is going away anyway. And as the poster says...

☆ ☆ ☆ don't let your fears ☆
       stand in the way, ☆
          of your dreams ☆
                ☆

.. So I'm not planning to.

I'm planning on taking Ben away some- where where we can have a bit of space, try new things and do what we want.

Hopefully Ben's mum will let us have
the car and then we can drive
somewhere.... maybe somewhere
romantic or by the sea like
Scarborough or Skegness. I'm going
to do some investigating.

♡ love ♡

Laura xxx

skegness

P.S If I'm back, I'll be able to sort
out the phone bill with
Daddy too.

Wednesday 22nd October
1997.

Dear Diary,

I'm in YORK! Took me ages to
get the feeling ☺ back in my left
leg after some fat lady got on at
Edinburgh and took up half my seat
for the rest of the journey. I just looked
out of the window and tried to listen
to my music. I really like the counting
Crows now.

Before I left the boys asked me how
long I was planning on being away
for.... probably so they could sub-let
my room or something not because
they care. I told them to stop
pretending to care and I might never
come back, then left after locking
all of my food + kitchen stuff in my
room.

I managed to book a room in a hotel
called the 'Sunningdale' in Skegness

It sounds really nice, full english breakfast is included and there's tea + coffee making facilities and a hair dryer in the room.

Hope Ben likes it. I had to put a deposit on my credit card.

I'm going to turn up and surprise Ben after he finishes college tomorrow I can't wait to see his face :)
I'm going to wear the shiny trousers he likes!

Sarah said that it sounded like we're going on some kind of dirty weekend away. I explained it wasn't like that that makes it sound cheap and this is something different because we're in L♡vE and anyway we're going midweek not at the weekend.
✦ I'm really excited ✦

It feels right that I'm home.
This is where I belong.

I'm going to phone Ben's mum on
the sly in a bit and see if we
can get the car, then I'll have
a bath, shave and pack a bag...
.. but if the break turns out the
way I want it to then I doubt
we'll need many clothes !!

love

Laura
xx

P.S. Wonder what Ben will
think about my bald
patch?

Friday 24th October 1997.

Dear Diary,

Ben's asleep - we didn't leave our room for the whole of yesterday... apart from when Ben went out to get some 'supplies'

When we checked in the guy kept calling us Mr + Mrs Sayers... had to try really hard to keep a straight face .... Its obvious what we're here for! The room is OK we've run out of tea and coffee though cos we didn't let them in to clean the room this morning.

Haven't seen much of Skegness yet and it was dark when we arrived so I think we might go out later, when he wakes up, to get some food.
          I'm starving!

Feeling a bit funny really. It feels like no one can touch us here and that we've really got space to be ourselves and do what we want. It's so nice to see him again and we're having loads of fun but I'm feeling a bit rejected. I told him I loved him last night but he didn't say anything back. He just kissed me on the forehead and said that he knew. Not really the response I was hoping for. All that can mean is that he doesn't love me.....

...then either I'm wasting my time or he's one of those boys who has a real problem saying it or he loves some one else?

Maybe he still loves
                    jenny?

If he still loves jenny then maybe I should come clean
            about Alan?

Then we can work through our
 problems together and make our
relationship work?
 I really don't know what to do
or whether I should even bring it
up at all?

Unless I give him some time and ask
 about it later on

Maybe he didn't even hear me
properly when I said it? He was
 quite tired.

 love
 laura
 xxx.

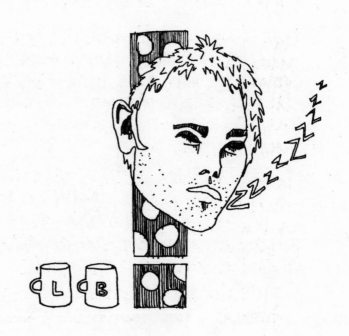

Sunday 26th October
1997.

Dear Diary,
Just passed Newcastle. The trains
quite quiet actually which is good
cos I'm sure my make up is
smudged. It's raining and it
feels like I'm in a film but a film
without a happy ending.... why do
I always cry on trains?

Had a really lovely time in Skegness...
made me think how great things
would be if it was just me and Ben
all the time, without hassles, without
Uni. Think we could have a really
happy life together.

Talked to him about the 'I love you'
thing last night. Felt I needed to
get an explanation. I asked him
when we were out at dinner so
that he couldn't strop off.
He said saying that got you into
trouble + just complicates things.

I don't understand how that makes
things complicated ... surely its
the most simple thing in the world?
He said that I don't love him, that I
just think I do and that actually
I'm in love with the idea of
being in love.

How does he know how I feel?
Maybe he's just one of those guys
that shows how he feels more
physically?

... Like I got him a kiss me quick
squeeze me slow hat that he
kept it on most of the weekend
... even in bed! and he won
me a teletubby out of a machine
in the amusements. Don't think
its a real one cos it hasn't got an ariel
but its the thought that counts.

Don't want to go back but suppose
I have to.. its not that long til the
xmas holidays love laura x PS. WONDER HOW
ALAN IS?

Wednesday 29th October 1997.

Dear Diary,
　　　Just got back from hanging
out with Lisa + Lin after Univat the
GU Bar. They're deal nice. Spoke to them
about Ben. Got a letter from him this
morning that really annoyed me. At the
end of ☆ the letter, instead of writing
　*　☆　*"lots of love from Ben"*☆*
like he normally does, he signed off with
　　　'lots of affection'
　　　(not love)　Ben'
How the hell is that meant to make me
　feel?
Lisa ·thinks he's had a bad experience
in the past and that I need to help him
through it. I put the fake teletubby he
got me in the bin and I'm ⌐not
going to write to him for a while
⌐and see how he likes that

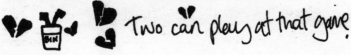　Two can play at that game.

I decided I ought to channel my efforts into something else so got an application form off Fraser for Sub city in English.

Lisa and Lin said they'd do it with me. Hopefully they'll give us a show. Imagine how funny it'll be!?!

Think the boys must be trying to cook, cos the flat stinks of fish. Melanie from upstairs has been hanging out in here a lot. I think she might have snogged Alan when I was away, she's always in his room I'm not jealous.
I'd just appreciate it if someone had the manners to actually tell me.
Sleazy Alan's in the kitchen, so I'm just going to go to sleep now.

P.S. Do the couple upstairs ever stop!   = Really not in the mood
love laura x

Thursday 30th October
1997.

Dear Diary 🌸

🌸 Didn't go to Uni as the flat needed
cleaning — lets face it the boys
wern't going to do it.

Sleazy Alan came in and said he wanted
'to chat'. I really couldn't be
bothered with him and asked him
to go but he kept following me
wherever I went and wouldn't leave
me alone.
The only way to get away from him
was to lock myself in the
shower. I must have been in there
for about 45 minutes. He just kept
telling me that he liked me.
        I just kept telling him to
            get lost.
After a while I got out of the shower +
knee'd him in the nuts. He's so

annoying. And he smells. I think
he got the hint eventually.
Just in case I locked myself in my
room until the boys came home.

Dave and Alan have just been down
to have a word with him. Apparently
he won't be bothering me again.

All I want to do is phone Ben but
I don't want to give in —
anyway if he doesn't love
me then he won't care.

Dave and Alan will look after me.

love

Laura xxx

P.S. I'm never taking a day off uni
again!

Monday 10th November 1997

Dear Diary,

Had our first Subcity show today. Got all the CDs ready last night. I was dead nervous so we met in the GU bar before and I had a couple of pints

We decided to call ourselves

'the L team'
as all our names begin with L
(laura, lisa + lin)

There were loads of scary people hanging around the studio when we got there, being all cool but they left after about ten minutes into our show. I don't think they liked what we were playing I was quite glad cos they were putting me off.

It was really nerve racking if you think about it, broadcasting to the **WHOLE OF GLASGOW** and surrounding area... that means a lot of people listening to us!

I tried not to think about it.

We said we'd do requests and dedications but no one really called. Fraser said they'd been having problems with the phone so it could be that again but if it wasn't not to worry cos not that many people listen at that time.

I made a few mistakes but all in all I thought we sounded very professional. I was glad I was with lisa and lin for my first time.

Just phoned Ben and he wants me to send him a tape as he thinks it'll be an interesting listen. He's being dead supportive and that makes me love him even more but obviously I would never tell him that!!

Maybe he's just being nice cos he thinks I'll be getting loads of male attention now that I'm on the radio?

love
Laura
xxx

P.S Maybe Uni isn't as bad as I thought.

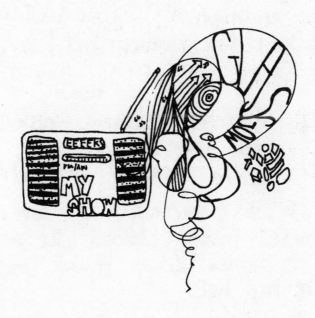

Monday 17th November
1997

Dear Diary,

Mr Sandman. Bring me a dream
Make it the sweetest that I've
ever seen! — sorry It's in my
head.

I've had the farts all day, finished
my essay, did some laundry,
had a drink ... Bob's your uncle.

Sarah was wearing a dress over
trousers today, looked like she
was a dinner lady. I think I might
have told her.

The boys said I was being very
funny. I tell you, put me in a
room with me and I'd have a
right laugh.

Phoned Ben earlier, he seemed a bit

quiet, remember talking to him about jenny. He said my accent has changed. I can't remember much more about the conversation

Tamsyn was funny lady in the Teletubbies today. Tinky Winky collected songs in his gay bag and Po chored Laa-Laa's ball. I've decided Dipsy is crap. All that stuff he does with his hands when he walks makes him look like a teeny bopper trying to dance in silks. Big green waste of space

My writing looks funny.
love laura x

P.s I think I'm going to buy a plant.

Tuesday 18th November 97.

Dear Diary,
    We christened today...
'NATIONAL HANGOVER DAY'
Didn't make it into lectures... my brain
won't work.

Ben just phoned. He was in a right
mood. He said I kept going on about
Jenny last night + that he didn't
enjoy speaking to me at all.

He says things have got to change.
I said "what like my accent?"
but he didn't find it very funny.
Seriously, he needs to chill out,
he's like my bloody dad giving
me lectures like that.....
    what's he going to do next?
                Fine me?

All I wanted was for him to be nice
for me. I had a headache before
but he's just made me feel a million
times worse.

I hope he feels guilty about being so
nasty. I only share my insecurities
with him about Jenny cos he's
out with her all the time and
you're meant to talk about stuff in
Adult relationships for them to
work, especially long distance adult
relationships.

I know that you understand, you
always do and never answer
back. I thank you for that.. a real
friend.

Me + Sarah are going to get chips +
cheese in a bit. She hasn't said
anything about the dinner lady
thing THANK GOD! I don't think
she remembers! love laura x.

Wednesday 19th November
1997.

Dear Diary,

Sorry if my writings funny but I'm
crying.

Ben's dumped me. Got a letter from
him this morning. I feel so empty.
My heart aches and my throat
and eyes hurt cos I've been
crying so much.

I tried to call him but his Mum
says he doesn't want to speak
to me. I feel all ~~choked~~ choked
like I can't breath without him

I just don't know what to do ;

     . . .

I know he was annoyed the other night but I didn't think it was this bad.

He said I'd changed. That he couldn't cope with my constant paranoia and that he couldn't deal with such an intense relationship with his mocks coming up.
  I'm at University for Gods sake .... Surely its intense for me too but I can handle it.

I finished his painting today too. I feel like ripping it up into a thousand pieces cos that's what ~~it feels~~ it feels like he's done to my heart. ♡

Bens jumper doesn't even smell
of him any more and even
photos don't look the same. I
keep looking out across all the
lights of the city + thinking
about how far away he is and
if it would all be different
if I was still in York.

Why did this have to happen?
I can't do this by myself.
I love him and I don't think he'll
ever understand how much.
He was the one who made me
happy + now he's gone.

I just want to speak to him
I've never felt this about anyone
and its killing me   love laura
                              x.

Thursday 20th November 1997.

Dear Diary,

Can't stop listning to Counting Crows, can't stop thinking about Ben. He was the only person who truly knew me. Feel really lonely, really anonymous. Feel like walking into a pub and shouting

"I bleed too"

but I doubt anyone would notice...

You get friends for reasons, friends for seasons and friends for life but none of them understand what I'm going through. Its ironic that the 1 person who would understand is the reason I'm falling apart inside.

I don't think Im ever going to stop loving him

We break up in a couple of weeks.
Going home is going to be really
hard. Everything reminds me of
him, the places we went, the
silly things we joked about, the
times we spent together.

Everyone seems to be all happy in a
relationship. Mr X is seeing someone
and even Mel and Alan got together

I just don't know how things can
change so quickly, the week before
he was going on about buying
me new underwear and now
this

I want him back. I don't want to
grow up to be one of those old
ladies with loads of cats!

love laura xxx

10th August 1998

Dear Diary,

I knew things would be better when I got back from Uni. Ben seems a lot more chilled out since his exams finished. I just hope he gets the results he needs.

Debbie gave me a payrise at the hotel to £4.50 an hour, should be able to save a bit but not as much as last summer cos of the summer rent on the new flat — worth it though when I move in.

Going swimming at the Barbican tonight with Ben. Its part of our new fitness thing. Its always a bit embarrassing. I hate walking out of the changing rooms. Everybody looks at me. I think

I need to get a new costume.. Its a
bit tight now. Think my boobs
must have grown or something.
The materials gone all funny +
see through where it's stretching.
I thought you were meant to
stop growing after puberty?
They better stop soon or its going
to be ridiculous. Ralph keeps
making jokes about me not being
able to see my own feet.

Ben has started calling me "chumpy"..
He says it doesn't mean anything
and it's just affectionate. I think
it sounds like a chubby name...
like when you call people "bubbly"
but you really mean theyre fat.
Maybe thats why he's so keen we
go swimming all the time.
I might start calling him
"little one" just to be affectionate and
see how well that goes down. laura x

11th August 1998.

Dear Diary,

Ben came round straight from work today and so had a shower at ours. Daddy was in a right mood about it and kept going on about how he found it intrusive and he shouldn't be made to feel like that in his own house. I didn't say anything.. but surely its more intrusive that he walks around in his nightshirt all the time, especially when he sprawls out on the floor in the lounge and you get an eye full of things you really don't ever want to see —

now THAT'S intrusive —

what a bloody hypocrite Its not worth it anyway. He's always criticizing me whatever I do.
I'm used to it.

His favourite line at the moment is that I'm treating the house like a hotel.... Well guess what? — thats exactly what I'm doing. I wouldn't be there if I had a choice I'll be back in Glasgow in a couple of months!

I think Mary's crush on Ben is getting worse. She won't leave him alone. She made him a card.. Its got lots of hearts on it and she's signed it "Love from Fox Mary"... .. She really is a freak.

Its good though cos she'll do her Ace Ventura impression whenever Ben asks.. Its hilarious!

I asked Ben if he thought my boobs were getting any bigger but he said he hadn't noticed.. but he's always telling me that I

shouldn't bother wearing minimiser
bras and that I should just embrace
my body.

Vic called from Glasgow. She said
kirsty has decided she's a lesbian.
To be honest I always knew she
had it in her.
          She does look like one anyway.

Anyway I'd better go. Ben's trying
to get my attention by sticking
his finger in my ear.
      He reckons he's got something
        to show me...
                    ♡
                ♡   ♡
                  love
                ♡   laura
                    xx ♡♡ ♡
                      ♡♡ ♡   ♡

✽ ✿ ✽ ✿ ❀ 14th August 1998.

Dear Diary,

❀ ✽ ✽ Ben took me to Harry J Beans
last night – its well posh. We had
two pitchers of Miami Dolphin because
I was too embarrassed to ask for sex on
the beach. They only cost £4.99 cos
it was Happy Hour.   When we
moved on I started buying him
doubles but didn't tell him. I like
it when he's drunk cos he's more
affectionate! ♡

I'm so glad we sorted things out.
This summer would have been
crap without him. People at work
are always commenting about how
good looking he is and say I'm
really lucky that he's going out
with me. ♡ ✽ ♡ ♡✽

✽ ☆ ♡ I just love him so much ♡✽
✽ ♡ ♡ ☆ ✽ * ♡
✽ ✽ ☆ ☆ ☆ ♡ * * ♡

I feel really proud that he's my boyfriend. He's got strong legs like a carthorse and when I'm with him my head feels all heavy like I'm intoxicated with Love...

I know it sounds stupid but I'm sure I'll marry him one day. I think Laura Clarke sounds nice and it looks good when you write it too...

Laura Clarke L Clarke.
Laura Clarke.

L Laura Clarke

L Clarke Laura Clarke

laura
Clarke Clark laura Laura
Clarke. Clarke Clarke.
laura Clarke

L Clarke.

L Clarke x

Got a new swimming costume today - had to get a size 16 as all the smaller sizes wouldn't fit around my chest. I decided to weigh my boobs on the scales in the bathroom I put them on the side of the bath and did it that way.

They weigh about 1 STONE !!! That's like 1 tenth of my body mass. So actually if I was flat I'd only weigh 9 stone.

love

Laura xx

P.S. Ben's taking me to Sheffield tomorrow to see the Owls play.

P.P.S We watched a programme about a cellist called..

..YO YO MA
Ben thinks the name's hilarious!

☆
☆Dear Diary,   19th August 1998.

     Me and Ben ended up in Silks with
Ralph and his new girlfriend last night.
I haven't met her before. I think
she's a bit weird. She was wearing
a cropped tassly top, knee high boots
and hot pants and took me into
the toilet to show me her tattoo of
a mushroom on her hip, its horrible.

It was a good night though. I had
7 bottles of hooch. Ralph was doing
his Boyzone dancing and Ben was
wasted. I had to put him in a
taxi home after he was sick on me.
Not feeling the best today. Decided
to come clean and tell Daddy
that I smoke socially sometimes when
I'm at the pub. I wanted to be
honest about it incase someone sees
me and reports back to him. I shouldn't
have said anything. He told me

I had let him down, that he expected more of me and that he hadn't paid for me to go to private school for me to throw it away by developing filthy habits like smoking.

He said I should consider my actions carefully whilst staying under his roof. I pointed out that he smokes sometimes like when he has cigars at Christmas time. He said that was different. God knows how. I was only trying to be honest. I've been listning to the last mix tape Ben gave me and I've just realized the last song on it is U2 – still haven't found what I'm looking for.

How am I meant to take that exactly?

Do you think he's trying to tell me something?

I thought the last song on a mix tape was always a really significant one

and if thats the case then according
to him, me and Ben have no future
together.
          I thought we did..

My head hurts. I don't know why
I bothered getting up today...
I don't think anyone appreciates
how hard it is being me.
I try to do the right thing but
     I never get it right
    What's the point?

              love

          Laura x

21st August 1998.

Dear Diary,

I really don't know what to do.
Ben was being quite restless in bed
last night — I thought he was
having a bad dream but then
I'm sure I heard him say...

"Charlotte..."
He kind of groaned it so I may not
have heard him properly but I'm
almost positive he did.
What the hell Am I meant to do?
First the mix tape and then this...

I didn't say anything about it cos
I didn't want to start an argument—
he would only deny it or he won't
even have realized he did it in
the 1st place. I think he knew
something was wrong when I left
but I couldn't face talking

to him about it. I was scared about
what he might say. I don't want
us to split up again.

The only Charlotte we know is Callum's
girlfriend. He may have been dreaming
about being out with them
or something?
That's not so wrong. I mean I always
dream about weird people. Doesn't
mean I fancy them does it...so why
should this situation be any
different?

I can't lose him now. What if he
was thinking about her though?
What if he fancies her?
She is quite pretty if you like that
kind of thing but I think her
eyes are too close together.

Maybe I'm being paranoid?

I don't know anymore.

P.S It's just been announced
Posh Spice is pregnant.

I'm not sure I can cope with all this
I'm trying to be rational but every
way I think about the situation
ends in me being alone again

I can't win

I'm never good enough am I?

love

22nd August 1998

Dear Diary,

 I've just got back from a long walk
in the rain. I needed to clear my head
I'm soaking but I don't care. It felt
good just standing there getting
wetter + wetter.   Nothing between
me and the sky, my naked soul
fully exposed to the elements.
 I came in though cos I started to
shiver and then Daddy told me off
for dripping water + mud up the stairs.

 I've been thinking about me and Ben
a lot. I looked in my dream book
and it doesn't look good. The book
helps you interpret   your own
dreams rather than   what you
hear someone saying in their sleep
but I think its still accurate..
 It says if you hear your own name

called there's important news to
come but if the call you heard was
for someone else then the news is
likely to involve a divorce or break
up of some nature.

When I was in the rain I thought
about the Spice Girls a lot.   I realized
I need to have more self respect, more
girl power and that if I don't confront
him I wouldn't be being true to myself.

In 'Stop' the words go 'slow it down, read
the signs so you know just where
you're going'....
                    So thats what I'm
                    going to do.
I'm going to tell Ben what I heard
and ask him if he fancies Charlotte
then I'll know once and for all.
Geri left the SG's and they were Ok..
So if Ben leaves me I will be too.
          I deserve to know
                    love laura x.

Dear Diary,

I feel so worthless. My eyes sting from crying too much and I know I'm going to get told off cos I've just noticed I've got mascara all over my duvet cover.

I met Ben in the Fleece for his lunch break and I asked him about Charlotte. It was really quiet in there but I knew it needed to be done. I didn't want to make a scene. I finally got it out and Ben got narky and denied everything

He then told me he couldn't cope with my constant paranoia and that he'd been meaning to tell me he's decided when he goes away to Uni he'd like to go as a single man.

What the Hell !?!

23rd August 1998

Firstly I know what I heard and
secondly where the **HELL** did that
come from?

How can he plan that and expect me
to be fine with it?

How am I supposed to act for the rest
of the summer..
              ..LIKE **EVERYTHING**S OK?

How am I meant to feel when I know
that with everyday that passes it gets
closer to the day that he's going to
turn around, go off to uni and leave
me behind?

I know that going to Uni is a big thing
and I know that he wants to do
well but I managed it. I spent the
whole of my 1st year going out with
him and doing the long distance
thing — why can't he do that?

Why did I have to say anything?

I'm always the one that messes things
up. Why don't I just think before
I open my big gob then none of
this would have happened?

I'm in a relationship with no future
I feel empty. Its like working for
no money or like making the
tastiest chocolate cake you've
ever seen and then not being able
to eat it..

Whats the bloody point?

laura
x

31st August 1998.

Dear Diary,
 I've decided there's only one
thing I can do and that is to make
Ben change his mind.
I've booked a hair appointment at
Harland's to get my highlights done.
I'll buy him presents and I'll do that
thing he's been wanting me to do for
ages. I'm going to be the best girlfriend
 ever.

I am a woman with a mission and time
is my enemy.

He means far too much to me to lose
him now. The thing that upsets me
most is that he's willing to give up everything
we have, everything we've shared just
so that he can enjoy some
cheap tart during freshers week,
              guilt free.

To think that I sacrificed the whole

of my first year at uni for him makes me sick (snogging Alan doesn't count cos I only did it cos I was missing Ben)

I need advice from someone a bit older and wiser. There might be something obvious I'm not thinking of and its always good to get another perspective I can't ask my Mum cos it would gross me out too much and things were a lot different in the older days so I've decided to write to Mel C.

The SG's are always so confident. They are experienced women of the world and I know they wouldn't let anyone walk all over them. They've probably had loads of boyfriends so would know exactly what to do in my situation.

Mel always seems so sweet and all the other girls go to her for advice so I don't think she'd mind too much if I asked her.

I've got the address of the fan club
and I know that they always pick
up their mail so I'm gonna do it
I know she'll be able to help me.

love

laura

P.S Wood Pigeons
are so annoying.

1 September '98.

❋ Dear Mel C,
❋ I hope you're Ok.
First of all I just want to say I
think 'Viva forever' is a brilliant
song and Congratulations on
your No 1.
    I hope you don't mind me
writing this letter. You don't know
me but I've been a fan of yours
(and the other girls of carse!)
since you began. I'm not a stalker
or anything so don't worry.
    I know you must get a lot
of mail but you said on

live and kicking recently that
you enjoy reading it and try
to reply to as many people as
you can, so I guess thats why
I'm writing.

If you haven't got time then
don't worry but I want you to
know that this is really important
The Spice girls have enspired
me for a long time. Your music
has really touched me and
often when I'm unsure of what
to do I ask myself...

What would a Spice Girl do?

This time I'm asking you directly
cos its a bit more complicated.
 I need some advice.
Basically Ben (thats my boyfriend)
made me a tape with 'I still haven't
found what I'm looking for' on it
by U2. Then I heard him saying
another girls name in his sleep
and I asked him about it but
he said it didn't mean anything
but then said that he wants to
be single when he goes to University.
 The thing is, that makes it
sound all really black and white
but its more complicated than that

cos I really love him and think
we might get married but we
can't do that if he dumps me
when he goes to uni. I was hoping
that you might be able to offer
me some advice about what to
do, like how can I make him
change his mind?
    I really need you to help me.
I'll do anything. He does love me,
I just don't think he realizes
    how much yet.
    Thankyou for taking the time
to read this....

... if you're ever in York or Glasgow give me a call.

I look forward to hearing from you.

love

Laura (Sayers)

xxx

P.S Congratulations to Posh + David Beckham... just think a real baby spice!

8th September 1998.

Dear Diary,

Ben said Charlotte again in his sleep last night. When I heard it I felt sick. Once is bad enough but twice?!?!! What is it about her

She is NOT even Pretty!!!

I can't say anything cos if I do then Ben might just say lets end it now. Maybe she's been flirting with him? Maybe she secretly fancies him? What the hell gives her the right to flirt with **MY** boyfriend and manipulate him like that?

No wonder hes saying her name in his sleep, she's poisoned his mind..

SHE IS EVIL

Sometimes I feel we're so far apart
But you're always in my heart
You are always on my mind
I know you find the words are hard to find

I've never felt like this before
And I've never felt so sure
I worry and panic that I'm not right
I think of you when I'm alone at night.

Are there others you much prefer
Who's advances I should deter
Knowing exactly what they say
Tempting you while the cats away.

I know I'd be stupid not to give this a go
But its just so hard when you say there's no
tomorrow.
Why do you say the name of that Harlotte
Do you have a hidden love of Charlotte?

I do believe in what will be will be
And we may split up when you go to Uni
But not before I have tried all I can
I am your lady and you are my man.

               love laura x

P.S Mel B is Pregnant too now.

*   9th September '98

Dear Diary, ☼ *

☼ Ralph just gave me a croggie
back from town. I decided Callum
had a right to know what has been
going on. If my relationship is
going to suffer because of his
stupid girlfriend then quite frankly
his can too. Its only fair. ☼

I may have made it sound a bit worse
than it actually is by saying that
I knew she'd been flirting with him
but lets face it, just saying Ben had
said her name in his sleep, twice,
wasn't going to get the results I needed.
☼
I think I got the point across. Callum
didn't seem happy at all when I left
him. Maybe he should have thought
about that before he started
dating someone like her. They say
you should never trust someone
who's eyes are too close together
anyway. ☼

I told him I'd appreciate it if they could give us a bit of space whilst we were trying to sort things out and he said he would and thanked me for letting him know.

I feel better. If Ben does fancy her a bit then there's no way anything can happen now. Even if Callum asks Charlotte about it, she denies it and they carry on going out, Callum will always be wary while Ben's around.

Now I've solved that little problem, all I have to do now is convince him to stay with me when he goes to uni.
   I love him so much.

                love laura
                        x

P.S Still no reply from Mel C yet. ♥

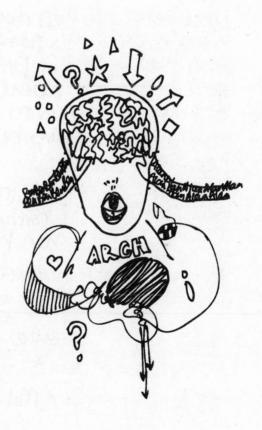

11th September 1998.

Dear Diary,
        I think I'm pregnant and I
really don't know what to do. Ben
stayed over last night. We are always
careful. Ben is dead responsible like
that, that's one of the reasons I love
him so much but last night it went
wrong.

We called the family planning centre
and they're not bloody open today!
Going to the drop in centre tomorrow
Ben says he'll go with me. Think
he's as scared as I am. It's going
to be embarrassing. I know
 everyone will be looking at me,
making assumptions, judging me.

It's horrible, I just want to die, it's not
as if we were being stupid. If we
were then I'd deserve this but we
weren't and I don't.

I want to tell my mum and have a big cuddle but I can't. I want to phone Ben and talk to him about it but our parents might hear so I can't.

I suddenly feel very alone. I keep thinking about the science lessons we used to have at school. All those pictures and diagrams. I keep touching my tummy. There is a baby forming inside me right now and I'm scared.

I haven't smoked all day just in case and I know it sounds stupid but I'm scared to go downstairs in case my mum can tell. What if she can tell? kind of like womans intuition.

I can't have a baby now. It would change everything. I've got yonks left at uni. I haven't got much money. I know that my boyfriend is going to dump me in two weeks time + daddy will go mental.
     This is not what I need now
P.S Still no letter from Mel C.   laura x

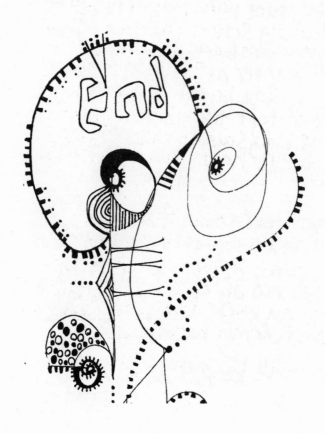

13th September 1998.

Dear Diary,
    I've been sick all day.
    I feel horrible.
Took the day off work (they are not
happy.) and went to the family
planning place with Ben. We felt
like naughty school children. They
give out numbers like at the
cheese counter at Safeway. Ben
stayed outside while I saw the
nurse and I got the morning after
pill. the lady said to take one,
then wait 12 hours then take the
next one.

I couldn't even get that right. I
really tried not to be sick as i
know I can't be pregnant and I've
got to get rid of it now before it
gets any worse but I felt awful
and my tummy was churning

    I couldn't keep it down.

Ben was really sweet about it but I can tell he was worried. I'm going to have to go back tomorrow, explain what happened and get some more. You can only take it for 72 hours after – what if I throw up again? Then what do I do?

I feel tired and upset. I'm writing this from my bed. Daddy always says that bed is the safest place in the world but it doesn't feel that way now.

Mama thinks I've got food poisoning and Mary keeps asking me why I'm crying. I want to tell them so I don't feel like this by myself. I just want everything to be ok and back to normal.
I can't do this.. I don't feel strong enough
I'm scared .. really scared
love Laura x

13th September 1998.

Dear Diary,
        Its 9pm now and so far so good.
I've got to take the second tablet at
midnight and I haven't been sick
yet. The nurse told me to take it with
food and that I was probably sick
cos I took it on an empty stomach.

I saw Ralph in town and told him
where I was going cos he said I looked
awful. I wish I   hadn't cos he
went mad and said he was going
to have words with Ben as
    'nobody does that to his sister'
Typical over protective brother —
    managed 'to persuade him
that braying Ben wasn't going to
help   matters.

When I got back Mama told me she
    knew. I shouted at her for having
the nerve to read my diary,

then she told me she'd seen the
packet for the tablets on my bed
so I had to tell her what happened.
How could I have been so careless?
    Well done Laura... Actually she's
been ok about it. She brought me
a hot water bottle and made me
soup and told me she was proud of
me for acting so responsibly.
        Responsibly?
Surely I wouldn't be in this mess if
that was the case? It was like she
was trying to bond with me or
something.. 'women together'
but to be honest it just grossed
me out.

I just have to stay up to take this
tablet now and that will be that.
I just want it to be over. Get back
to work before I get sacked
and get back to normality before
I go mad.

Ben has been so great. Really supportive.
It just made me think about
how much I love him and how much
its going to upset me when we
break up. We've been through
such a lot together - Good times
and badtimes, plus he knows me
inside and out! !!!

We've got a history but no future
and that kills me.
I'm just so tired.

love laura
X

P.S Still no reply from Mel C.

14th September '98.

Dear Diary,
Do you know what? I've had it
with Ben... in fact I've had it with
men full stop. Being a lesbian seems
a very good option right now.

What kind of boyfriend hangs up
on you? Why does he have to
be "so horrible"?

I love him so much and I'd never do
anything to hurt him and then
he turns around and accuses me
of making the whole pregnant thing
up?!! How can he possibly think
   that? How can he think that I
want a baby now?!

He said I'd been acting strangely
for a while and he wouldn't put
it past me that I had manipulated
this whole situation so that he
couldn't go away to uni as a single
man. Seriously what kind of

person would be that devious? He can't think much of me if he thinks thats the case... and that makes me sad. Yes I love him and yes I was desperatley trying to convince him that we shouldn't split up but it looks like thats going to happen anyway.

He said that if I was willing to go to such lengths then I'm not the person he thought I was. I told him he was being unfair that of course I don't want us to break up but I'd never do anything like that! I don't want to be tied down either. Then he made some comment about me being obsessed and suggested I was copying the Spice Girls....two of them are pregnant so obviously I thought it was a good idea too. Oh please! He's talking like I'm some mental fan. I like their music

and I think they're great but I do
know the difference between
fantasy and real life!

I can't do this anymore.. Its just
too hard. I'm not sure whats going
on. I'm not even sure if I still have
a boyfriend. Everythings gone
wrong. I just want it to be like it
was before.. We were so happy
How can you think someone knows
you so well but they obviously don't
know you at all?

I feel hollow.. I can't eat.. I feel sick
My heart aches and I've got a snotty
nose cos I've been crying too much
my entire world has fallen apart.

love laura x

P.S Daddy has just told me off for leaving
the emersion on.

17th September '98.

Dear Diary,

Excuse the writing but I've had some cider and I don't care. Ben hasn't spoken to me since the other night and if he hasn't already decided the whole thing is over then I BLOODY WILL.

I spoke to Vic and she made me see how stupid this is. I'm tired of feeling so down, so upset and so worthless. She said there's someone out there who will love me and treat me like a princess. I don't need to be made to feel like this. I'm worth more than this. I am a good person and I have a lot to offer a man. I don't know why I haven't realized it before but I am a total walkover – even Ben said I'm a doormat – even I know thats not good

Well this is it. From now on I'm a new Woman. NO MORE doormatting for anyone.

Ben can go away to Uni as a single man with my bloody blessing. I don't know what he thinks its going to be like... some kind of meat market I suppose. I hope for his sake that it is! I hope he gets off with loads of women... I hope he makes loads of friends and has a really bloody good time.

But you know what? I know he'll miss me but he's got to realize that himself and until he does I'm not going to be fully appreciated as a Woman.

I need to have more self respect...
more

R.E.S.P.E.C.T.

What will be will be. I'm not loving
someone who doesn't love back
That's crap.
   I might as well love a carrot....
I might get more love back from a
                    Carrot!
          Or a parrot .. they can talk.

Still no reply from Mel C but she's
probably very busy. Anyway I reckon
I'm doing what she would have
told me   to...

        GIRL
        POWER!
                love
                Laura
                   xx

Final Thoughts.

October 2006.

Its now 8 years since that last entry and I still write my diary every day. To have my deepest thoughts from my formative years broadcast on the radio and now published in a book though is a very strange feeling.

Quite why so many people have been so hooked on my embarrassing trials and tribulations is a bit of a mystery to me. All I can guess is that a lot of people have all been through the same thing... first kiss, first love, long distance relationships, emotional insecurity, and even a worrying obsession with the Spice Girls.

A lot of the people from the diaries I catch up with when I go back to York. I still talk to Ben and luckily he doesn't mind the details of his love life being exposed for all to see as well. Despite what I thought back then I did manage to get over him.

Today things are more stable in my love life but getting here was even more weird than I could possibly have imagined.

Inspired by my stunning lack of success in the boy department, Scott Mills and my team at Radio 1 came up with "One night with Laura" ... an X-factor style search of the UK for my Mr Right. And that's how I met James. It's always very interesting when we meet people for the first time and they ask us how we met....

"He won me in a competition"

I find works the best.

Will it end happily ever after?
I guess we'll find out in my
future diaries.
But I'm planning to keep them
well hidden

love

Laura xx

P.S Mel C never replied.